Contents

Words that are printed in bold, **like this**, are explained in the glossary on page 31.

Amazing woodlice!

Have you ever seen woodlice? Woodlice are flat creatures that scurry in dark, damp places. You may have seen many woodlice in a compost heap, among dead leaves or under a pile of wood. Perhaps you have seen one curl up into a ball. When you look at them up close, woodlice really are amazing animals.

Woodlice are often found in large groups under logs.

Woodlice
Up Close

Greg Pyers

Raintree

www.raintreepublishers.co.uk

Visit our website to find out more information about **Raintree** books.

To order:
- ☎ Phone 44 (0) 1865 888112
- 🖹 Send a fax to 44 (0) 1865 314091
- 🖥 Visit the Raintree Bookshop at **www.raintreepublishers.co.uk** to browse our catalogue and order online.

Published in 2005 by Heinemann Library
a division of Harcourt Education Australia,
18–22 Salmon Street, Port Melbourne Victoria 3207 Australia
(a division of Reed International Books Australia Pty Ltd,
ABN 70 001 002 357).
Visit the Heinemann Library website at
www.heinemannlibrary.com.au

First published in Great Britain by Raintree,
Halley Court, Jordan Hill, Oxford OX2 8EJ,
part of Harcourt Education.
Raintree is a registered trademark of Harcourt Education Ltd.

℟ A Reed Elsevier company

© Reed International Books Australia Pty Ltd 2005
First published in paperback in 2006

ISBN 1 74070 235 2 (hardback)
09 08 07 06 05
10 9 8 7 6 5 4 3 2 1

ISBN 1 844 43808 2 (paperback)
10 09 08 07 06
10 9 8 7 6 5 4 3 2 1

Editorial: Anne McKenna, Carmel Heron
Design: Kerri Wilson, Stella Vassiliou
Photo research: Legend Images, Wendy Duncan
Production: Tracey Jarrett
Illustration: Rob Mancini

Typeset in Officina Sans 19/23 pt
Film separations by Print & Publish, Port Melbourne
Printed and bound in China by South China
Printing Company Ltd.

The paper used to print this book comes from sustainable resources.

National Library of Australia Cataloguing-in-Publication data:

Greg, Pyers.
    Woodlice up close.

    Includes index.
    For primary students.
    ISBN 1 74070 235 2. (hardback)
    ISBN 1 844 43808 2. (paperback)

    1. Isopoda – Juvenile literature. I. Title.
    (Series: Minibeasts up close).

595.37

Acknowledgements
The publisher would like to thank the following for permission to reproduce photographs: © Steve Hopkin/ardea.com: pp. **12–13, 19, 24**; © Dwight Kuhn: pp. **6, 22, 23, 27, 29**; © Naturepl.com/ Niall Benvie: p. **10**, /© Dan Burton: p. **7**, /© Duncan McEwan: p. **26**; Lochman Transparencies/Dennis Sarson: pp. **8, 18**, /Jiri Lochman: p. **14**, /Peter Marsack: pp. **4, 28**; photolibrary.com: pp. **15, 16**, /SPL: p. **11**; © Paul Zborowski: pp. **5, 25**.

Cover photograph of a woodlouse reproduced with the permission of Naturepl.com/Niall Benvie.

Every attempt has been made to trace and acknowledge copyright. Where an attempt has been unsuccessful, the publisher would be pleased to hear from the copyright owner so any omission or error can be rectified.

There are more than 3500 kinds, or **species**, of woodlice.

What are woodlice?

Woodlice are crustaceans. Crabs, crayfish and barnacles are also crustaceans. Crustaceans have no bones. Instead, they have a hard, tough skin, called an **exoskeleton**. Crustaceans have many legs and most kinds live in water. Unlike most crustaceans, woodlice live on land.

Other names

Woodlice are also known as slaters, sowbugs and pillbugs. One of them on its own is called a woodlouse.

Where do woodlice live?

Woodlice are found in many different parts of the world. They live in the hottest deserts of Africa and in salty pools in Australia. The common sea slater lives on beaches. Most woodlice live in forests.

Habitat

A **habitat** is a place where an animal lives. Woodlice are found in a lot of different habitats. Most live in damp, dark places. The **leaf litter** on a forest floor is a good habitat for woodlice. Woodlice are also found in compost, soil, and under bark and rocks.

The cracks in brick walls can be home to many woodlice.

Woodlice that burrow

Desert woodlice dig burrows to shelter in during the hot day.

Woodlice live in these places because they find their food there. They can also stay hidden from **predators**.

Many woodlice move out into the open at night to feed. During the day, beach woodlice shelter under rocks, seaweed and driftwood. They come out to feed when the sun has set.

Living in dark, damp places keeps woodlice from drying out.

Woodlouse body parts

A woodlouse's body has three main parts. These are the head, the **thorax** and the **abdomen** (<u>ab</u>-da-men). The body is covered by a hard **exoskeleton**.

The head

A woodlouse's head has a mouth, two eyes and two pairs of feelers called **antennae** (an-<u>ten</u>-ay). One pair is very small and difficult to see.

The thorax

In adult woodlice, the thorax has seven parts, or **segments**. Each segment has a back plate. These look like pieces of **armour**. The woodlouse's seven pairs of legs are attached to these segments. A pair of legs is attached underneath each segment.

The abdomen

The abdomen is much shorter than the thorax. At the end of the abdomen there are two tail-like body parts called **uropods**.

Woodlouse colours

Many woodlice are dark grey in colour. But there are also red, orange, brown, cream and green woodlice. Some even have spotted skin or a stripe.

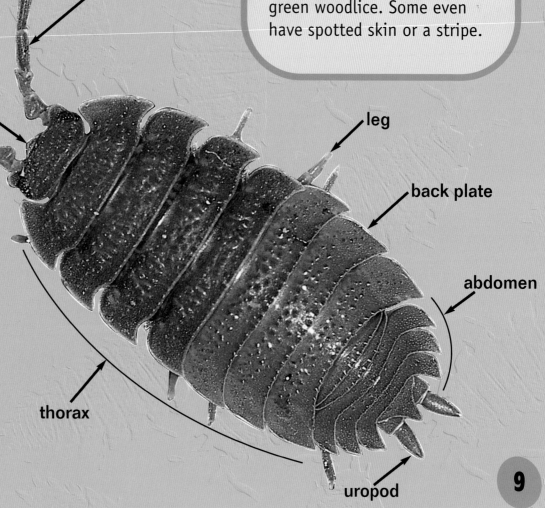

antenna

head

leg

back plate

abdomen

thorax

uropod

Mouthparts and eating

Most woodlice eat rotting plants. In a compost bin, woodlice eat potato peelings, cabbage leaves, tomatoes and carrot tops. Woodlice also eat **fungi** that grow on leaves. Quite often, they eat their own droppings.

Woodlice sometimes eat the flesh of dead animals. They may eat other woodlice, even when they are alive. This may happen when a woodlouse is shedding its skin. At that time, its soft body is easy to bite.

On a forest floor, woodlice eat dead leaves and wood.

Mouth

The mouth has two jaws, called **mandibles**. These break food into small pieces for swallowing.

Drinking

Woodlice get water in several ways. One way is from the moist food they eat. Another is to drink it, for example, from dewdrops. A third way of getting water is by taking it in through their **uropods**.

A woodlouse's mouth is underneath its head.

mouth

Droppings and nutrients

Woodlice recycle their waste by eating their droppings.

Why do woodlice eat droppings?

When a woodlouse swallows food, the food moves through a long food tube to the stomach. As it moves along, the food is broken down. This releases **nutrients**, which the woodlouse needs to stay alive. The nutrients are taken into the woodlouse's blood. Some nutrients may pass out through the anus in the woodlouse's droppings. By eating the droppings, a woodlouse can obtain these nutrients.

Copper

One nutrient a woodlouse must have is copper. Copper is a metal, like iron or aluminium. The copper in the woodlouse's blood carries **oxygen**. Woodlice get copper by eating rotting leaves. When there are no rotting leaves about, a woodlouse can get copper from its droppings.

Blue blood

In human blood, it is iron that carries oxygen. Iron gives our blood a red colour. In woodlice, copper gives blood a blue colour.

Rotting leaves supply copper for this woodlouse.

Seeing and sensing

Woodlice **sense** the world around them in several ways.

Eyes

A woodlouse has **compound eyes**. Each compound eye is made up of many very small eyes. Each small eye faces in a slightly different direction. It sees something a little bit different from the other eyes.

Some insects' compound eyes have thousands of small eyes. A woodlouse's compound eyes have just fifteen to twenty small eyes. This means that a woodlouse's eyesight is poor.

compound eye

A woodlouse does not need good eyesight because it lives in dark places.

Folding antennae

When a woodlouse rolls into a ball, it neatly folds away its antennae into hollows in its head.

Antennae

A woodlouse has two pairs of feelers called **antennae**. One pair is large. As the woodlouse walks, it taps these antennae on the ground in front of it. The antennae pick up smells and enable the woodlouse to find food. Smells can also lead a male woodlouse to a female.

The second antennae, called **antennules** (an-<u>ten</u>-yools), are tiny and probably have no use.

A woodlouse uses its large antennae to find food.

antenna

15

Legs and moving

Woodlice have fourteen legs. The legs are arranged in seven pairs. Each pair is attached underneath a woodlouse's body. There is a pair of legs attached to each of the seven **segments** of the **thorax**.

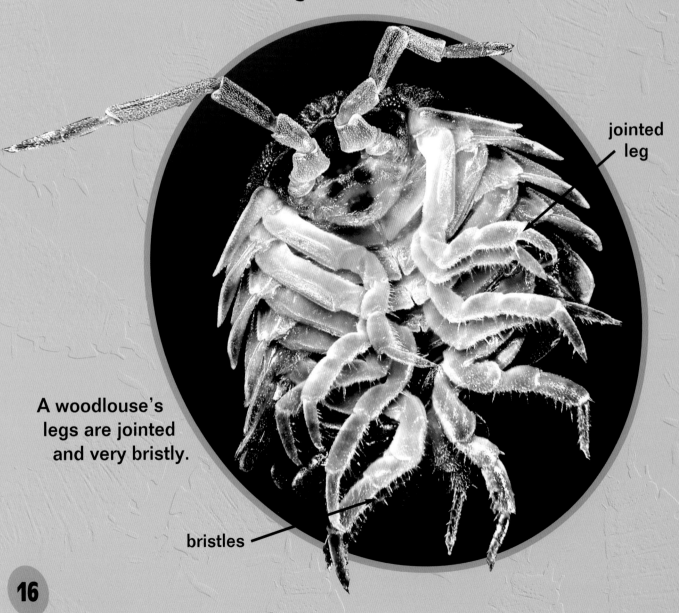

jointed leg

A woodlouse's legs are jointed and very bristly.

bristles

Legs

Woodlouse legs are jointed. This means that they have separate sections joined together. All fourteen legs are the same size and shape.

Walking and running

Woodlice can move at different speeds. When they are searching for food, they move slowly. When a light comes on, or when a **predator** is about, they scurry for cover.

A woodlouse does not walk just on its feet. Half of each leg also touches the ground. The lower part of each leg has short bristles. These give the woodlouse a good grip on leaves, rocks and sticks as it walks.

Protecting themselves

Many animals eat woodlice. There is a **species** of spider that eats nothing but woodlice. Centipedes, beetles, frogs and newts eat woodlice. In Europe, hedgehogs and shrews eat woodlice.

Avoiding predators

One way that a woodlouse avoids **predators** is to hide. Some woodlice scurry away when danger threatens. Others can roll into a ball. This protects their soft undersides from attack by small predators, such as centipedes. Rolling up may also confuse a predator.

Woodlice can give off an unpleasant smell. This keeps many predators away.

A pillbug is a woodlouse that can roll into a ball. The other woodlouse pictured cannot roll into a ball.

Drying out

Many species of woodlice lose water quickly through their **exoskeletons**. Their exoskeletons are not waterproof. But this is not a problem as long as these woodlice remain in damp places.

Desert woodlice avoid losing water by staying in their burrows by day. They come out to feed after dark.

Inside a woodlouse

The inside of a woodlouse is a lot like the inside of an insect.

Blood and heart

A woodlouse's blood moves through the spaces in its body. The heart is long and tube-shaped. It runs beneath the **exoskeleton** along the woodlouse's back. Blood travels from the head, through the **thorax** and **abdomen**, then the heart pumps it forward again.

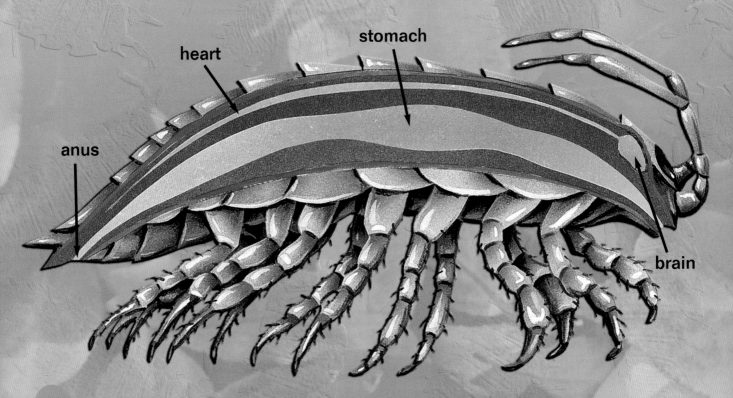

heart

stomach

anus

brain

20

How do woodlice get air?

Woodlice do not breathe air in through their mouths. Some **species** take in **oxygen** through groups of tiny tubes underneath the back end of their bodies. Other species take in oxygen through **gills** under the abdomen. Inside the body, oxygen is taken into the woodlouse's blood.

The brain

A woodlouse's brain gets information that it **senses** through its **antennae** and eyes. It sends messages to the rest of the body about what to do.

Woodlouse eggs

Woodlice hatch from eggs in a pouch under the mother's belly. The eggs start to develop there after she **mates** with a male woodlouse.

Life in the pouch

Dozens of eggs may hatch inside a woodlouse's pouch. But the babies do not leave the pouch. They stay there to grow and develop. The pouch is full of **fluid**. This stops the babies from drying out.

Woodlouse eggs do not have shells.

This woodlouse is carrying eggs in her pouch.

The pouch is above the first five pairs of the mother's legs. The top halves of these legs lie quite flat against the pouch. They protect the pouch from damage if the mother walks on rough ground or rolls into a ball.

Leaving the pouch

After one to three months, the young woodlice are ready to leave the pouch.

Producing alone

The females of some woodlouse **species** produce young without **mating** with a male.

Leaving the pouch

At first, baby woodlice look very much like adult woodlice. There are a few differences. They are much smaller and much lighter in colour. This is because their **exoskeletons** have not yet hardened. Young woodlice have only six pairs of legs.

These young pillbugs stay rolled up to protect themselves from **predators**, such as centipedes.

Growing

At this early age, young woodlice are called **mancas**. Within a day of leaving its mother's pouch, a manca has grown too big for its exoskeleton. It **moults**, which means that the old skin splits and the woodlouse crawls out with a new, bigger exoskeleton. After the second moult, the woodlouse is called a **juvenile**.

A juvenile woodlouse has seven pairs of legs.

Getting bigger

As a woodlouse grows to adult size, it **moults** several times.

Moulting

Moulting takes place in two stages. First, the **exoskeleton** covering the rear of the woodlouse loosens. This makes one half of its body paler than the other half. The exoskeleton splits and the woodlouse pulls itself free.

This woodlouse has just moulted the front half of its exoskeleton.

The second stage follows a few days later. The exoskeleton covering the head and first half of the woodlouse's body falls off.

Dangerous time

Moulting is a dangerous time for woodlice. This is because the new exoskeleton is soft. Until it hardens, it provides little protection against a **predator's** jaws.

A moulting woodlouse may be attacked by several other woodlice at the same time.

This woodlouse will now eat its old exoskeleton. It uses the **nutrients** in the old exoskeleton to grow a new skin.

Woodlice and us

Woodlice cannot bite or sting. They do not carry diseases that make people sick. They do not harm people at all. They break down dead plants and compost to make **fertile** soil. But still, most people do not like woodlice. Why?

Maybe it is because woodlice have many legs and remind us of spiders. Perhaps it is because woodlice are seen in dark, damp places where there are rotting plants. These are the kinds of places people do not like.

Woodlice do an important job in compost bins, breaking down food scraps.

Woodlice make good pets

Some people keep woodlice as pets. A plastic or glass container with some soil, dead leaves and a few twigs makes an excellent woodlouse **habitat**. A spray of water now and then will keep it moist. The woodlice can be given a few pieces of fruit or vegetable peel to eat.

You can learn a lot about woodlice by keeping them in a jar or box.

Find out for yourself

You may be able to find some woodlice in a garden. Look in the soil, among the **leaf litter**, and under rocks and logs. You could keep some woodlice in a container (see page 29) and watch them up close.

Books to read

Looking at Minibeasts: Crabs and Crustaceans, Sally Morgan (Belitha Press, 2001)

Heinemann First Library – Bug Books: Woodlouse, Stephanie St Pierre (Heinemann Library, 2001)

Using the Internet

Explore the Internet to find out more about woodlice. Websites can change, so do not worry if the links below no longer work. Use a search engine, such as www.yahooligans.com or www.internet4kids.com, and type in a keyword such as 'woodlice' or 'woodlouse', or even 'sowbug', 'pillbug' or 'slater'.

Websites

http://www.geocities.com/CapeCanaveral/Hangar/7649/wlice.htm
This site has lots of information about the bodies, behaviour and **habitats** of woodlice.

http://www.allaboutnature.com/subjects/invertebrates/isopod/Pillbugprintout.shtml
There are facts about woodlice and a labelled diagram for you to print out at this site.

Glossary

abdomen   the last section of a woodlouse's body

antenna   (plural: antennae) feeler on a woodlouse's head

antennule   small antenna of a woodlouse

armour   hard covering that protects the body

compound eye   eye made up of many small parts

exoskeleton   hard outside skin of a woodlouse

fertile   having many nutrients

fluid   something that is runny, not hard, such as juice

fungus   (plural: fungi) plant-like living thing that feeds on dead plants and animals

gills   body part of some woodlouse species that allows them to breathe

habitat   place where an animal lives

juvenile   young

leaf litter   dead and rotting leaves on the forest floor

manca   young woodlouse before it moults for the first time

mandible   jaw

mate   when a male and a female come together to produce young

moult   when a growing woodlouse splits open its exoskeleton and climbs out of it

nutrients   parts of food that are important for an animal's health

oxygen   gas in the air that is needed for life

predator   animal that kills and eats other animals

segment   one of the separate parts of a woodlouse's body

sense   how an animal knows what is going on around it, such as by seeing, hearing or smelling

species   type or kind of animal

thorax   chest part of a woodlouse

uropod   short tail at the rear end of a woodlouse

Index